# WHOLEHEARTEDLY

# IN LOVE

## SHADONNA STARKES-CLEMONS

Cover Design by Shariva Smith
Editing, Interior Design and Layout by S. Michelle LeSuer

Library of Congress Cataloging – in – Publication Data: 2024945451

ISBN: 979-8-9880673-1-3

PRINTED IN THE UNITED STATES OF AMERICA

Writing is a form of euphoria for me

Writing allows me to step temporarily step into another world

The poems allowed me to transform into a world of love and intimacy and put it all on paper

I hope those that read this collection allow themselves to step into that world and let your mind explore

Enjoy!

Warning: If you are not comfortable in the skin you're in, uncomfortable reading about love, sex or erotica, do not continue. If you are not ashamed, then please continue.

When I put this together, it was done so with all of that on my mind and in my heart. Pure and unadulterated…

Shadonna Starkes-Clemons

# Our Love

My love for you is strong

Your love for me is long

Together we are one

You and I under the sun

When I think of what we share

There is nothing else to compare

You give and I take; You take, and I give

Our love is anything but fake

True love is something we have

Shown always through the love we make

This poem was written as a token of my love for you

With the question in mind; without your love

What would I do?

So, let's stay together bound by the heart and make a vow to never part

# Shadonna Starkes-Clemons

# The Way You Make Me Feel

The way you make me feel

You really turn me on

The things you do keep me going

My cookie gets moist with the mention of your name

I massage your back with oil

From there I caress your loins until you boil

Ooh! You beg me to stop there, but I go faster with longer strokes

Faster and faster I go until you grab my hair

That along with your moans let me know you're ready so I prepare

Up and down! Round and round! Left and right!
Which lasts a few moments

And then we explode all over each other

I look in your eyes and smile thinking to myself
**Damn! I love this man!**

And that is how you make me feel

# My Promise of Love to You

I promise to kiss you hello each time you come home and goodbye each time we leave each other

I promise to listen to you and try to understand your feelings even when they're different from what mine would be

I promise to be your biggest fan and support you in all you do
I promise to laugh with you at least once a day

I promise to hold you in my arms every night and tell you how much I need the closeness we share

I promise to love you with all my heart, and to never stop finding ways to show you how much
I promise to be there for you always being your shoulder to lean on

I promise to talk to you even when I may not want
to talk

I promise to do all these things and more today
and every day as your wife

# Don't Take Your Love Away

Where would I be without your love?

You must have been sent from Heaven above

You look at me and my insides melt like butter

I look at you and your heart begin to flutter

The love we share is undying

The time we have is limited

I hope that within time our love surpasses life's ups and downs

Turning the frowns into smiles at all times

In denial for so long

It took a while to realize where my heart really lay

You have changed my whole life

And I look forward to your smiling face every
single day

I wonder from time to time about how it came to
be

But then I say to myself, "don't question the
inevitable"

As they say, "what's meant to be will definitely
be"

I thank the Lord for allowing it to be me

You are so fine you blow my mind

When you were created you were one of a kind

Everything about you is pleasing to me from
your head to your toes

The spell you have on me nobody really knows

Don't ever take your love away

## Wholeheartedly In Love

I'm here to stay always

With you as long as you allow me to provide the
kind of love, I know I'm capable of giving

Shadonna Starkes-Clemons

# We Are One

When I think of you; I think of me

You and I together represent we

We are one; You and I having fun

All day long together we are under the sun

One is a word meaning single

Thinking of us as one has a different meaning

One for us is togetherness

One for me means loving you only

One for you means not being lonely

You are the bright spot in my life

One day I hope to be your wife

## Wholeheartedly In Love

Lil momma is what you call me

With you always is where I want to be

We are one you and I

We are one a star in the sky

One meaning you; One meaning me

Together as one we will be

Shadonna Starkes-Clemons

# Making Love

I want to feel your hands all over my body

I want to feel your lips on mine

Up and down, round and round

From the sky to the ground

Bump and grind, moan and whine

My body shivers from the touch of your hand

You continue daily to blow my mind

Without a doubt you're one of a kind

Touch me, feel me, and caress my every being

In return, I'll make you feel like you're a king

Ooh! Ah! Ooh La! La! Is what you'll say

Cat and mouse is the game we'll play

## Wholeheartedly In Love

I'll pour chocolate on your chest

You'll lick the whip cream from my right breast

Your body all over my body

We'll be like a hot toddy

You slowly enter my warm cove

If only you knew the emotions, you drove

As you rock my world, I start to scream

Slowly afterward I tremble and then cream

The bed shakes like an earthquake

When it's over, my legs begin to ache

You kiss me gently on my neck and I kiss you
back with a peck

My head rest on your chest

Sleep creeps up on us and out we go both with a
smile

Knowing that the love we made was the best

# Untitled (Feelings)

Why do I feel the way that I do about you?

What is it that makes me care so deeply?

In all my years I can honestly say that this

Is the deepest I've felt for someone in a long time
and you were never actually mine

All I want to do is love you

Allowing me to love you is what I want in return

Without your love I keep asking myself, "What
am I to do?"

You don't know it, but you play a very important
role in my life

I believe in my heart if I pray hard and long
enough, one day I may just be your wife

## Shadonna Starkes-Clemons

You are to me like the air I breathe; hard to live
without

I can say now that I love you without a doubt

There are times when I can't sleep for thinking
about you

Then I ask myself, "What am I to do?"

Why can't I be with you?

Is it that you don't want me?

Are you not ready to give me what I want?

Or is it that I'm not good enough for you?

Then I say to myself, does he really know how I
feel?

If he doesn't, what am I waiting for to let him
know the deal?

Once again here I go jumping out on a limb

## Wholeheartedly In Love

I'm always going out on a whim but as Toni says,
"I Love Me Some Him"

I'm on my journey to never-never land

Trying to come back with my man

Don't you understand?

He'll be mine; I'll be his; and this is the way my
life is

Shadonna Starkes-Clemons

# Weak

I get so weak! Can I take you out tonight?

Those are the songs that make me think of you

You brighten my day and put a smile on my face


Our times are over now; happiness never lasts

My feelings for you are still here and alive

Your feelings for me have taken a deep-sea dive


I get so weak when I think about the notion of
being either with or even around you

Our ride didn't last long but it prompted a song

So, my next move is to stay strong

Do me baby is what I want to say to you

Love me body and soul is what you will do

Give me love; Give me affection

Take my body section by section


Friends we were Friends we are

Close I'll be Never too far

Always here to keep you near


You make me "weak"

Shadonna Starkes-Clemons

# Emotional Rollercoaster

You have me on an emotional rollercoaster

I wish on a daily we could be closer

What am I to do if I can't be near you?

Sometimes I sit back and cry, not sure of what to do


I've never doubted your feelings for me but sometimes I sit and wonder

Do you really want to be with me?

Is there really an us to be concerned about?


Loving you was never healthy

Loving you has never been easy

## Wholeheartedly In Love

Because of the love we have I make do

I make do because I love you

The rollercoaster has been a hectic ride since day one

Continuously up and down without the fun

As time goes on, I keep telling myself things will get better

My heart is holding on, but my mind is almost gone

What am I to do for the sake of loving you?

Honestly my ride is over

I can't go on like this anymore

My emotions can bear no more

So, here's my stop finally

Shadonna Starkes-Clemons

Always remember that I love you

And last but not least

You'll always be in my heart

# One Wish

If I had one wish it would be for life to be
perfect

If I had one wish the many struggles would be
well worth it

If I had one wish our love would be never
ending

If I had one wish you would be here with me

If I had one wish, I would prove my love so that
you can see that with you is where I'll always be

If I had one wish our always and forever would
be together

If I had one wish it would be that you loved me
always unconditionally

If I had one wish it would be for our hearts to
beat as one

If I had wish we would be happily laying out in
the sun

My only wish is that you know I loved you
despite everything and what we shared was
second to none

# Love

New love is beautiful love

Old love is trying love with great attributes

Your love for me has never faded

My love for you has been upgraded


To be with you again is wonderful

It takes my feelings to new heights

Never would I have thought after all this

Time apart the chance would come again


For us to be together as one

For you to be the one that will soon be my life
partner

Me your wife and you my husband is awesome


Being with you puts my mind at ease

I couldn't have imagined in the past you being
able to do that so effortlessly

You know me better than I know myself which is
greatly needed and appreciated


You and I are one and from now to forever

Together we will be having fun living life

You are my King and I your Queen

# Satisfaction

Looking at you gives me

Making love to you gives me

Being near you gives me

Thinking about you gives me


Oh, how I love the satisfaction you give me

Lay me down and please me as only you know
how

When we're done, I'm so sated all I can do is rest


I'm your favorite girl in the whole world

Your love and heart were given to me

Diamonds and pearls don't compare to the love
we share

Nothing else will ever be fair

Our eyes meet and from beginning to end there
is pure

"Satisfaction"

# Point of it All

I'm here for you

No matter what you do

My love gets stronger each day

You came along and stole my heart

Giving me a brand-new start

The love you give me is real

Hearing you confess your emotions only seal the deal

The ups and downs we go through make things a little rough

We fuss then break up to come back and make up

Telling me you love me I know it is true

Trying to get over the hurt but what am I to do

Shadonna Starkes-Clemons

Promising the good out way, the bad

I'm giving you the best you've ever had

Standing tall professing it all

The point of it all is writing on the wall

# Superman

You're my superhero

You're my world

There's no mountain that I won't climb

There's no bridge that I won't cross to be with
you

Being in your arms is like loving SUPERMAN


It's a bird it's a plane

I will be your Lois Lane

There's nothing else I'd rather do than be with
you

Looking into your eyes calms me

Your presence alone soothes me

## Shadonna Starkes-Clemons

The way that you do me moves me

Our love is powerful

The ever-present pull is willful

I promise to stay by your side

There's no need to hide

Being with you is like loving SUPERMAN


There's no hill that I won't scale

There's no light that I won't shine

Hearing you say "you are mine" was like music
to my ears

The passion behind your words

The way that you do me is like no other

Being in love with you is like loving SUPERMAN

Take my hand and you will find

A love like no other

I hope you feel it to

Waking up next to you is all I want to do

You're my SUPERMAN

Shadonna Starkes-Clemons

# Make Love to Me

Make love to me like only you can

Make love to me because you are my man


Our love is like no other

Two peas in a pod we are together


Sex is like none other that I've experienced

Passion beyond measure


Cookie leaking with pleasure

Waiting for you to reach the treasure

## Wholeheartedly In Love

My heart pounds with anticipation

Love so good I want to give a standing ovation


You're my heart and I'm your girl

Head so gone constantly on swirl


Slowly lay me down; turn my body around

Whisper in my ear; rub my kitten down


Make love to me, touch me, please me

Explore my body like a deep blue sea

Shadonna Starkes-Clemons

# Thinking of You

You are the air that I breathe

Wherever I am, Whatever I do

I think of you


No matter the time of day

You are with me in all that I do

I think of you


Everywhere that I go

Whether I have a smile or a frown

I think of you

## Wholeheartedly In Love

There are not enough hours in the day

To completely express all the ways

I think of you

You mean the world to me

Loving you is what makes me free

I think of you


At night all I want is you

There is no denying this love is real and true

I think of you


You bring me peace

You bring me joy

I think of you

My axis spins better when I'm with you

My heart beats to the rhythm of your voice

I think of you


My soulmate you are

You're never too far

I think of you

# SoulMate

Our love intertwines like a rope

Two hearts beating as one

The connection we share on a level beyond the surface

Loving one another mentally, physically, and emotionally

So in tune that your pain is my pain

Best friends and lovers without question

No denying the amazing chemistry

Sex so passionate you can't tell where you end, and I begin

Our thoughts alone should be a sin

Separated for a short time but not severing ties

## Shadonna Starkes-Clemons

Leaving fate to the open skies

A future so promising for a love so bright

Not new love but true love

Lovers and mates vowed to never dissipate

# Unconditional

Love without conditions

Unselfishly

Thoroughly

Completely

Accepted flaws and all

No matter what

Without Limitations

You love me affectionately

No boundaries

A love so absolute

Regardless of circumstance

Shared love so fleeting

Total acceptance

Conditionally

# Way to Your Heart

Teach me how to love you

Show me the way to your heart

Is there a guidebook to your love?

I want to know what makes you smile

Break down the wall that hides your all

Be free with me and trust I will never hurt you

Open up to me completely

My promise is to love you unequivocally

Lead me down the road to your love

Learn you and understand the words to your
song

Ultimately finding my way to your heart

# Love Is

Love is blind

Love is never ending

Love is enlightening

Love is a lesson learned

Love is unconditional

Love is sometimes overbearing

Love is family

Love is full of bliss

Love is peace

Love is two people building as one

Love is soul stirring

Love is stories untold

## Wholeheartedly In Love

Love is making memories

Love is romantic evenings

Love is musical

Love is believing

Love is and always will be you and me

Shadonna Starkes-Clemons

# Take Me Away

Take me away

Hold me in your arms

Promise to never let me go

You are everything to me

Your love will set me free


My love for you is real

I belong to you so tell me how you feel

Being with you is so good

Thinking about us always puts me in the mood


You say I am yours now and forever

## Wholeheartedly In Love

Reassuring me at all times

That your love is unconditional

Vowed to love one another flaws and all


Take me away

Whisk me away to the unknown

Anywhere with you is where I want to be

Me for you and you for me


Together until eternity

Under the sun gazing in your eyes

Destination after destination by your side

Having fun and loving with no regard

Our chemistry is amazing

Loving on one another

Carefree lying on a beach

Preparing our future

No questions asked except one

Can you take me away?

# You Bring Me Joy

You bring me joy

Every time I think of you

I smile and all is well

My heart swells at the mere thought of seeing
your face

No matter the time or place

Your comfort is all I need

You bring me joy

To know that surrounds me in peace

No one else can do what you do to me

When I am down the sound of your voice pulls
me up out of a dark place

Promise you will never go far away

Your love is here to stay

Hold me in your arms

Never let me go

This journey is all I know

You bring me joy

# Everything to Me

You're my best friend

The peanut butter to my jelly

Sometimes I don't know what I'd do without you

Not a day goes by that I don't think of you and smile


Some say I'm tripping

But I know what true love is

My heart beats rapidly every time you are near

Our love blows my mind and I never fear it ending


You cause me to feel this way

What more can I say

My love for you will never fade

I can say for certain that

You are everything to me

# Longing for Your Love

Stroking my kitty kat with you in mind

Wanting you deep inside me

Crying out while you bring me to the edge like
only you can

I feel you pulsating with each stroke

Oh, how I can't wait to drain you of every drop


The longing and pleading always makes it better

Around you I can't seem to get myself together

I'm so horny I can taste it

Pleasing myself while we're pleasuring one an-
other

Cum for me baby, cum for me now

Those words alone make me explode all over
myself

You quickly follow with an explosion of your
own

Laying still we struggle to catch our breath

The need, desire and wanting was all I imagined
it would be

As always you come through and seal the deal


With no words spoken our hearts communicate

Syncing one to the other together forever

Silence lingers then the soul rests

Leaving us to love one another at our best

# You

You entice me every time we touch

My body automatically reacts

One look is all it takes to get me started

Your words move me to tears

Your unconditional love erases all my fears

In my heart is where you are

No matter the distance you are never far

Love my pain away

Keep me in your arms

Hold me tight through the night

Together always never putting up a fight

Bonded from the heart til death do us part

Shadonna Starkes-Clemons

# You Can Do Damage

The way my body responds to you

Everything about me belongs to you

If only you knew the control, you possess

A subtle touch causes me to lose all my senses

My body betrays me each time you are near

An intimate kiss to my forehead is all it takes

That simple gesture can start an earthquake

In sync always whether together or apart

Your aura is so powerful it draws me to you as
soon as you are within distance

The low whisper in my ear sends shivers down
my spine

## Wholeheartedly In Love

Intense stares tell so much that we communicate
without words

Your eyes being the mirror to my soul

Never would I have thought I'd experience such
love

So pure so true so strong

You Can Do Damage

Shadonna Starkes-Clemons

# Drive Me to Ecstasy

He loves me

He ignites a fire in me that cannot be extinguished by anyone

His touch makes my body tingle

I'm always feigning for another dose of him

I'm an addict of his love and tender touch

His touch has my body doing things of its own volition

Take me on a sensual slow ride to ecstasy

He caresses me without even touching me

He knows how to speak to me without opening his mouth

He makes love to me without being in the same room

## Wholeheartedly In Love

He drove me to euphoria without an orgasmic
release

Loves me like there is no tomorrow

Setting my soul ablaze just by his look

My entire body shivers from your mere presence

Leaving me open to all you have to offer

Drive me to ecstasy until the wheels fall off

Shadonna Starkes-Clemons

# When We

When we touch it ignites my fire

My heart swells with all the love I have for you

The connection between us is stronger than the eyes can see

Rubbing your hands all over my body gives me goosebumps

When we make love I get so excited my button overflows

Touching, kissing and talking dirty until we're both exhausted

Resting in each other's arms listening to our hearts beat in sync

Dozing off while thinking about the next time when we....

# My Promise of Love to You

I promise to kiss you hello each time you come home and goodbye each time we leave each other

I promise to listen to you and try to understand your feelings even when they're different from what mine would be

I promise to be your biggest fan and support you in all you do

I promise to laugh with you at least once a day

## Shadonna Starkes-Clemons

I promise to hold you in my arms every night and tell you how much I need the closeness we share

I promise to love you with all my heart, and to never stop finding ways to show you how much

I promise to be there for you always being your shoulder to lean on

I promise to talk to you even when I may not want to talk

I promise to do all these things and more today and every day as your wife

I can't thank you enough for the support. I hope you enjoyed the poems and are feeling some love within your heart. If you would be so kind as to leave a review I would greatly appreciate it. This was just the beginning so stay tuned for more coming in the near future from Shadonna.

# Shadonna Starkes-Clemons